Want

By

Catherine Glenn

How could something be
so obvious, yet, so hidden at once

Please enjoy the following poems
(and a few other things)

Dedication

My thanks to Corinne, Jen, Andrea, Lilia and Bob for their constant help, support and encouragement.

And for my wife, Sue, without whom my world as I know it today would not be possible, this poem is, and always has been, now that it is twenty years later, for you ...

A preemptive apology, a year later

I want to apologize in advance of advancing
past the time when I'll forget to remember
who I am or who you are, or we are, every day.
That used to be a joke but is now my fear
having found the wish. I apologize
for wanting more memories to forget,
each moment a jewel to misplace.
And I hope I remember – now, and then –
that it is so easy to forget what it was,
and what it could have been, without you

For Sue

If only I could

If only the heat
and thickness of the equator
was all I knew
what would ice and snow
mean to me!?

If only I could
look beyond dreams
and fantasy
what would love
hold for me?

If only the sand
and white dryness of desert
was all I knew
what would rain
mean to me?

If only I could
let go of fear
and imagined control
how much passion
would there be?

If only I could
take a step
down a path
what would life
hold for me?

If only I could.

Vermillion:

A dark crimson
fought off by light
white of life and
day orange of fall
change against
past fading into night
through the color
of my eyes after
losing myself in lost.

Silence

I've sat in silence and listened
to the trees given voice by rain
a conversation changing each instant
but still quite the same

I've stood in silence and felt
winter delicately conquer fall, slowly freezing
a gently built cast multiplying the reflection of
night light lost in the death of a season

I've walked in silence and thought
more comfortable in resurrecting pain
turned to a past alive in shadows
than struggling in today, trudging, toward gain

I've lived in silence and life slipped by
as I floated concerned only with what I saw
nearby, misunderstanding the *all* of the river
the infinite intertwined parts, the inexorable draw

And still I loved in silence and then lost
dreams that may never have been real
mountains retreating unclimbed
what my silence cost

Cruising

1. Gay

Can we choose to love?
Can we choose to care?

Cruising parked cars, engines
quietly warming after midnight
strolls through a dance of glances,
new but familiar faces each night
through windows or clouded breath,
a hidden life too dark for trust,
but dark enough to trade life
for a moment, to touch, but
not to love or hold another's truth,
to walk further away, deeper
into the night, the search for variety,
each a new spice to keep the spaces closed,
loneliness alone, the questions not allowed
      Quiet.
      No sound of soul.
What music then fills these moments
when the heart is held in frigid embrace,
winter and summer, and the screen replays
the scene over and again, without love
what is the search for, where does the journey lead,
strolling alone or seated, cruising the parked cars?

Can we choose not to love, choose not to care
when we've all had a small part
in creating the loneliness there?

2. Straight

Can we choose to love?
Can we choose to care?

Cruising packed bars, drinks
slowly warming after midnight
strolls through a dance of glances,
new but familiar faces each night
through windows or clouded crowds,
a hidden life too dark for trust,
but dark enough to trade life
for a moment, to touch, but
not to love or hold another's truth,
to walk further away, deeper
into the night, the search for variety,
each a new spice to keep the spaces closed,
loneliness alone, the questions not allowed
       Quiet.
       No sound of soul.
What music then fills these moments
when the heart is held in frigid embrace,
winter and summer, and the screen replays
the scene over and again, without love
what is the search for, where does the journey lead,
strolling alone or seated, cruising the packed bars?

Can we choose not to love, choose not to care
when we've all had a small part
in creating the loneliness there?

Watching her wait (to die)

On the death of a word
I pictured us standing around a dictionary
open to the precise page.
Who would actually redact?
(if that word were still alive in our circle)
(What if it had never been alive in our circle?)
Or would it just happen and a space would appear
for a moment, before above and below would expand,
while the corners would remain unchanged unless
it had been a corner, unless it had been *just there*

A stone, anchored, what then?

If that word was known to all, and it should be,
so simple, really, though vital to even our standing
around thinking how could you redact that
tiny (smaller than tiny) word that underpins everything
brings meaning to life, brings death to death, how could you?

What happens if we allow it to die?
What happens when we give up and redact:
Try

After when

This night begins as any other night out:
shower, shave, choose your clothes
shoes, hair, makeup, jewelry, nails

      if there's time
a glass of wine
by yourself is not a crime
dinner alone is fine
all this as common as a simple rhyme

      there is an age when
      a girl, a woman, is not noticed

as she asks for a single table
has just one drink and reads a book
waits to order, adds desert after her salad
later, walks to stretch her legs and the moment

      there is an age when
      a girl, an older woman, is not noticed

returning through a hotel lobby
riding an elevator, walking long halls
gliding back to a room quietly

to sit before sleep, before a mirror
a time with two faces and a question
more accepted than answered

      there is an age when
      a girl, a woman, is.

Wisteria

there was some speculation
about her beginning
whether a bird had dropped a seed
in the normal fashion, in the way of plants
or had someone sown specifically

but, how ever it had been
she took him, the pine, to be her own
a spindly runner whose gait had been lost
whose arms flailed at air formlessly

together they had become sky

                              dusk
on those certain nights, lavender
color and fragrance mixed
it seemed there was a breeze
                              but gentle
and clouds not quite distinct
and at the edge   honeysuckle

What if we are like Pi?

What if we are like Pi:
each infinite and unique
each a definition
each a key to understanding
each

Never to be told

Her nipples were pierced
so were his, as they jaunted on TV
and, I noted, the suckling
would not work on them

an odd association though
probably it is a matter of closeness
a region always just below the surface
not quite consciousness but easily found

it had been just a moment
less than a minute in the middle of a long night
when her mother could not offer
whether by fear of intrusion or pain or both

her breast to her infant's mouth
hungry, the infant and he held each other
seeking the same closeness, sustenance

he wished parents could be generic
exchange roles, fulfill the need
when a child's face turns to a breast
even one flat and empty though filled

for just a moment
a matter of closeness
of love, never to be told

Want

It is not something to write in a notebook
as they had only been dreams for so long:
breasts, a nose, cheekbones, hips, maybe hands

and then there were the silhouettes
in dreams against a sunset or atop a ridge:
tall, small waist, gentle curves

until at the reading, she, the image, was real:
full lit, same height and that blonde that comes in shades
like golden wheat with wind blowing it to waves

all of the features except the waist and hips
hers: athletic, narrow, a biker, a runner, lover of water
hands that endeared soil, carted stone, yet

words fell from them, effortless cascades

she tried to hide
her blouse revealing a taut abdomen
inviting your head, closed eyes
to just breathe

as words fell

it was not a matter of having her
she offered, whether she knew it or not

no, it was not wanting her
it was just want

Lectio

Selected Scripture – Mark 4: 33 – 41

Begin with the picture on the wall:

A blue-gray house
not dissimilar to the water it overlooks
darker than the sky that looks upon it
with different grasses in different response to breeze
in different response to season
as a shrub leafless appearing dead
though growing as if from it
colored as if the fusion of twigs and branches
an extension of grass climbing the home
on a chimney that parallels far on the horizon
the single white line of a sail

Begin Lectio, try to clear:

Centering, the first thought:
there is a woman who told these stories
this story, confidently, to all the children
they entrusted her with His word and their children

At sea, a storm arose; yet she found love
in arms they said were forbidden
those of another woman

They were afraid and fearful of their ship sinking
They abandoned her while reaching for their children
sought to save their boat by casting her into the sea

Scripture, two readings:

Mark recalls how
they put out onto that sea, to cross
as He said they should
a distance that must have been blue-gray
even in sunlight without a storm
though a storm did come
with wind that blew white-capped waves into their boats
while He slept and they cried of perishing
He woke rebuking the wind and sea, "Peace!
Be still!" Then, turning to them, "Why are you afraid?
Have you no faith?"

Mark said He always spoke in parables
But explained everything in private to His disciples

The third reading:

"He woke and rebuked the wind
And said to the sea 'Peace! Be still!'
The wind ceased and there was dead calm."

I wonder which are the parables
or when they become parables
wish to see direction in His simple words

the sea accepts them, life accepts them
in their boats, as they are

what holds them on their journey?

The answer is in His question

The fourth reading:

"Have you still no faith?"

at His word – peace
stillness, calm accepted all

We are all made in His image
we all are
in His image

Peace. Be still.
Have faith.

End with prayer:

I hold up my sister who found love
where You put it, where You led her

I hold her up now as a house become a home
though with fewer paths leading through grass to her door

I hold her overlooking a sea that may find a storm
though a sea calm in our sight

I hold my sister and her love listening to the voice across the water
a single sail set on our horizon

Peace. Be still.
Why are you afraid?
No storm will hurt you.

I hold you up, my sister
I hold you up

For Rachel

15

Let me tell you

Let me tell you about my womanhood,
which has nothing to do with a wig, make up,
spike heels and hose or even false breasts
(and I know they make bras to cover those points)
but I was trying to make a point about *my* womanhood
which has something more to do with observing:

Her at poetry night as she fixed her hair,
Alzheimer's having taken memories and now her hands
though she still fought fiercely in her motions
placing combs and pins, pulling and knotting
to clear her face, to clear her eyes
to listen without obstruction about womanhood
from the heart of a doctor who cares for poor children,
beaten children, young ones left for dead, and dead
a mother they often never have, not deaf to their cries,
who understands about womanhood and what it means
to continue, to be that which continues
and to be that which feeds

Let me tell you about my womanhood
about the night I heard and felt it
another long night following other long nights
of a baby's crying, of a mother's exhaustion
of aching breasts, of can't (and I understand)
let me tell you about lit by a light, a room and a hallway away
a scream caught in my arms and a head that turns
and a mouth that seeks and finds not milk, just touch
the connection in the shared catch of a shuddered breath
in the 4 AM suckling of a dry chest
in a perfect tiny fingernail

Let me share with you my womanhood
which is understanding, touching, feeling,
holding, feeding, amazement, joy
what the world should be
all it ever should be
but it is not
so I, woman,
stand close

Hidden

There, in the oak, a flowering Japanese cherry:
Sweet blossoms, feminine angles, delicate extensions.

How could something be
So obvious, yet, so hidden at once?

For Emily

I came upon a stone on a mountain

I came upon a stone on a mountain, actually two stones that had, obviously, been one. I was walking up and said to myself that 1 should try this little path off to the side on my way down. I found the path led to nothing significant except that upon returning to the main track my sight was directed across and back a bit. I'd not noticed this stone in my hurry on the way up, it was only upon slowing down coming down that I saw her. She had been left there with all the rest, millennia ago when the last sheets of ice had either fled back north or just melted. I thought possibly in their flight away what had carved across the side of this mountain, or over her top, had dropped these tailings from a height and that's when she would have been split. But then others would have been broken, too, not just this one. No, it was obvious that she had been placed just so, with a smile, or a dimple or maybe a laugh line, staring up at the sun as the trees that shaded me that afternoon, the ancestors of those trees, would still have been seeds many flights of birds or gusts of wind away. And then the cycle of snow and ice and freeze and thaw would have begun and any ancient observer would have lost count, and interest, long ago with this five-foot ball of schist. But at some point, on some day, there must have been that single expansion of water taking definite shape and she could hold herself together no more. And you might think that like a tree falling there was a tumultuous sound, whether or not a set of ears were poised to hear, because if nothing else the physics would have been the same. But as I stood there with her, staring at her and her companions, noting she was the only one who had been wrenched apart, it occurred to me this instance may well have been different because she was, somehow, different while still the same. Because had that parting been loud, fast, short moments of fluid motion leaving an echo sounding back up from the lake a thousand feet below and a mile or two away, she would not have remained here like this: touching, holding on to something that had been, possibly saying, *imagine what was but look at the wonder that is*. I conjured a winter when the ice wedge won but she was still held together by that season's ice and snow around her. And it was only in spring – and it had to be in spring didn't it because spring is "new" – as the ice and snow slowly left to feed the forest and lake that both parts of her began to move, not quite as one but still together. One falling backward, a new face to the sun; the other falling forward, coming to rest on the edge of her other self, this new face prevented from hiding by the other new face now open to all. She was, in effect, still one but showing everything that she had hidden, everything that had always been there, everything that made her one.

I sit in darkness, walk in light

"But by the grace of God, I am what I am"
I Corinthians 15:10

I sit in darkness, walk in light
I sit in darkness, walk in light

The Reverend Swanson pleads
Place no smiley face on the wound!
We must see the boil, taste the puss!
He is nearly crying, his book of hate held high
Please, please no smiley face on the wound!

I sit in darkness, walk in light

Because I let my children read magical books
I must drown them, he commands
millstones about their necks
to give them time to feel *my sin*
saving them from my sin, their own inevitable sin

I sit in darkness, walk in light

After the meeting, the little lesbian girl
enfolds me, whispers to me, *how can you*
love me when you don't even know me?
My mother doesn't love me!
crying, then through tears
How can you? I love you!

I sit in darkness, walk in light

I teach your children
I love them, too –
the girls who love girls
the boys who love boys
and the ones who hide in darkness –

Because I, too, sit in darkness
walk in light, yet cast no shadow
because that which is "I", sits in darkness

I sit in darkness, walk in light
I sit in darkness, walk in light

For Catherine

What if Eve

What if Eve
had just been listening, intent
in conversation with the stream about water
of life with the earth, about giving birth
what if she was just speaking
to women about women

What if Eve
never actually bothered with the serpent
other than a nod of good afternoon
because she saw through his insincere hissing
dismissing him, understanding
his character as women do

What if Eve
had learned on her own the joy
in the blue sameness of a robin's egg and the sky
in digging her toes into earth's soft skin
in playing finger games with the stream
what if she did this without an apple

What if it was Adam
just a young curious boy
just as all young boys since
reckless and fearless
and lying when caught
blaming the girl

What if God saw all this
gave Adam, gave men
the opportunity to change, accept
their mistake but they did not
and they blustered their lie more loudly
covering their guilt with the serpent's knowledge

What if God touched Eve
an instant later for Him, millennia for us
gave her the gift of true knowledge
told her to rise and use it
told her to save His creation

What if Eve stands, listens, then speaks

Puberty, a reprise

This time
no trepidation
not unknown
nor unaligned
or crazy

this time
wonder and wondering
converge

this time
just one me
forever

A Comparison

my rhododendron freezes quickly and curls her broad leaves
un-sharpened pencils or cigars to some
those that know think the curls fill with small ice
crystals that thaw only slowly, preserving the leaf

...

you freeze quickly, she says, when you realize
then curl inside yourself to hide
so no one will know, you cover yourself
in ice that thaws only slowly, to safely preserve

...

each branch end is an unlit ornament
tipped with a tight green bulb
anticipating June
blazing violet

for Andrea – hope that even at eighty
there will come a day when she blooms
as her true self

Eighteen lines

Two years ago I told my best friends, a hetero married couple I'd known for close to fifty years, that I'm a trans person. They weren't surprised. They said they'd known for twenty-five years and had just been waiting for me to say something. A year later, the day the husband and I both turned sixty-seven, he told me I really needed to "invest in a training bra, or something, because you kind of look like a seventh grade girl who's starting to, you know ... grow." I said I'd go put something on under my polo shirt, smiling all the way to my room to rummage through my suitcase. They had been two of the first I'd spoken to in what came to be an eighteen-month-long coming out journey to nearly all of my friends and many in my family. As anyone who has done that knows, it is terrifying, because no matter how confident you are in believing these people you have known most, or all, of your life will still love you and accept you, there is always that nagging doubt you could be wrong, and they'll leave. It happens; though, fortunately, only twice for me.

Six months after the birthday incident, I was offered a part in a regional theater charity performance of Eve Ensler's play, "The Vagina Monologues." I was to be one of three trans women performing the segment titled, "They beat the girl out of my boy ... or so they tried." Coming out to those I knew was difficult, but I still felt a sense of control, as everyone agreed to keep the news among those I told, because I was still only "semi-out;" "semi" because I couldn't be out at work and had yet to tell my elderly and very conservative parents. But the play, performing in front of 300 people I didn't know, was going to be something altogether different; the illusion of control would vanish entirely. For the first time ever, I was going to be truly open to the world, just Catherine, not anyone else.

After my first pass through the script, I wondered if I was the best person for this play because I felt it wasn't my story. It was a story that definitely needed to be told, just not mine. I don't know why I thought that; maybe I just didn't want to remember the years of hiding and lying. Or, maybe, I felt guilty because so much of this hadn't happened to me. I was elated when I was assigned these lines:

> Got my first hormone shot
> Got permission to be myself[1]
>
> The feminine is in your face
> I lift my eyebrows more
> I'm curious
> I ask questions[2]

Of all the lines in the segment, I felt so comfortable with these, because they were me, even though my "first" wasn't a shot; it had been a pill, taken on my 64th birthday while sitting in my living room and holding my wife's hand. Those words spoke to a giant change in the lives of many other trans women, changes they had desperately wanted to make, to stop hiding behind a false masculine image. For me, though, it had just been raising a translucent veil that never really hid who I truly was if you knew me well enough and paid attention. My hiding had been in plain sight and to my friends, those thoughts or just feelings made sense now. And to myself, I made sense now.

Rehearsal was the first time in my life when I participated in an event where I knew no one and they all only knew me as Catherine. There were eighteen of us; a few who had acting experience, most who did not, and a few who were petrified at even the thought of speaking to an audience. But they all thought this play was more important than their fears. They were to be the voice of the voiceless, and they welcomed me as one of those voices, as well. No one looked at me askance or mis-gendered me. I was, in their eyes, fully female. In fact, conversations were no different from what they would be at any party or gathering I'd ever attended had I'd been born female.

"You're a teacher? Tell me about that? How is it teaching young kids these days? That's a really pretty dress. I love your earrings, where'd you get them?" I was truly myself, nothing hidden, no acting, no affected voice or concern about the length of my hair. I was just me, all of me, and they embraced me immediately. It was, in a word, affirming.

Eve had written this monologue for five voices, but realizing finding five trans women might be difficult, the director was given the latitude to assign lines based on the number of voices available. There were three of us, and at our first rehearsal (we only had two) we took turns reading different lines, so the director could decide which lines to assign to each of us. The first three times through our part of the script, I did not read the final passage, eighteen lines that were not me, lines that frightened me, lines that required so much more than I thought I had within me to give. When the director finally asked me to read them on our last pass, it was all I could do to muster any voice at all.

> *I live now in the female zone*
> *but you know how people feel about*
> *immigrants.*
> *They don't like it when you come from someplace else.*
> *They don't like it when you mix.*
>
> *They killed my boyfriend*
> *They beat him insanely as he slept*
> *With a baseball bat*
> *They beat this girl*
> *Out of his head.*
>
> *They didn't want him*
> *Dating a foreigner*
> *Even though she was pretty*
> *And she listened and was kind.*
> *They didn't want him falling in love*
> *With ambiguity.*
> *They were scared he'd get lost.*
> *They were that terrified of love*[3]

29

After rehearsal ended, the director said she would look through the entire segment and work out how she wanted to pare five voices to three, and would send us an email with our parts in a few days. That was Sunday. On Tuesday I was assigned not only the lines I felt spoke about me, but the last eighteen, as well.

Eve interviewed scores of trans women before writing this monologue. Everything she wrote was said by one of those women, even the last eighteen lines. Everything is true. Even the last eighteen lines. True. There are people in this world (in the play those swinging the bat were soldiers) who not only want to kill me because I am trans, because I am an "Immigrant," but also someone I love, who just might, against all odds, love me, too. I have always known this sort of hatred exists. I hear it nearly every day in the news, in conversations with people who don't know about me as I move through the world even today in stealth mode. I know I have no legal protections to keep my job if I'm found out. In many states, if I were dating and surprised my companion with my "trans ness," and he "lost control" because of fear and killed me, the "trans panic" defense would justify the homicide. I have even heard the loathing from the pulpit of my own church, not from my minister, but from a church member who garnered applause and support for his comments.

Eighteen lines brought screaming home to me everything I have to fear. Eighteen lines brought a woman I'll never know into my arms, wanting to comfort her from thirty years away for the unfathomable pain of her loss. But there was just one line that voiced something I didn't know until I read it aloud:

> They were that terrified of love.[3]

Was that it? Were they terrified of us, all of us who are trans, all of us who dare to admit we have been created this way, only because we have all been taught not to love something defined as "different?" Is this why it has been so hard to learn to love myself?

On the night of the play, I held my script in front of me, (we all had to read from our own copy of the play, even though most of us knew the words) and I became her. To be sure, I shed tears as I read, and there was a break in my voice as I remembered a violent death I'd not known until I'd read the script the week before. And we, the woman from thirty years ago and me, tried to tell them, the audience and my fellow actresses, why it had happened, what she had finally figured out, but that's so hard to do in just eighteen lines, in just one line. I hope they understood. When I finished there was just silence.

The applause came some moments later, but my time had been suspended. I was standing there with her. She wasn't saying anything; she was just there. I felt her drawn back to a moment she had never left. There were two of us now, not one. She stepped a bit away, and I was left forever changed. I thought back then to what had been my trauma before, and I cried, embarrassed by the comparison. I warmed, smiled and cried at the miracle of friendship in being told to buy a training bra at 67. The applause faded, not because it had ended, but because there was no room for it, as the entirety of my life crashed in instantly, almost crushing the breath out of me, as I realized how much I owed this woman and all of those like her, unimaginably brave all. Eighteen lines, ninety- four words. I was forever changed. Light beckoned me from shadow.

[1] *Ensler, Eve, "The Vagina Monologues", VDay February 2020, Dramatist's Play Service, Inc., NYC, NY (2020) "They beat the girl out of my boy .... or so they tried" "Woman 5" pg. 15.*
[2] *Ibid., "Woman 1" pg. 16.*
[3] *Ibid.,"Woman 1" pg. 17.*
Essay previously appeared in Schuylkill Valley Journal, 2020

www.ingramcontent.com/pod-product-compliance
Lightning Source LLC
Chambersburg PA
CBHW051741040426
42447CB00008B/1255